FINGERPICKING STANDARDS

ISBN 978-0-634-06536-1

Visit Hal Leonard Online at www.halleonard.com

This book not for sale in the EU.

HAL•LEONARD®
CORPORATION

7777 W. BLUEMOUND RD. P.O. BOX 13819 MILWAUKEE, WI 53213

INTRODUCTION TO FINGERSTYLE GUITAR

Fingerstyle (a.k.a. fingerpicking) is a guitar technique that means you literally pick the strings with your right-hand fingers and thumb. This contrasts with the conventional technique of strumming and playing single notes with a pick (a.k.a. flatpicking). For fingerpicking, you can use any type of guitar: acoustic steel-string, nylon-string classical, or electric.

THE RIGHT HAND

The most common right-hand position is shown here.

Use a high wrist; arch your palm as if you were holding a ping-pong ball. Keep the thumb outside and away from the fingers, and let the fingers do the work rather than lifting your whole hand.

The thumb generally plucks the bottom strings with downstrokes on the left side of the thumb and thumbnail. The other fingers pluck the higher strings using upstokes with the fleshy tip of the fingers and fingernails. The thumb and fingers should pluck one string per stroke and not brush over several strings.

Another picking option you may choose to use is called hybrid picking (a.k.a. plectrum-style fingerpicking). Here, the pick is usually held between the thumb and first finger, and the three remaining fingers are assigned to pluck the higher strings.

THE LEFT HAND

The left-hand fingers are numbered 1 though 4.

Be sure to keep your fingers arched, with each joint bent; if they flatten out across the strings, they will deaden the sound when you fingerpick. As a general rule, let the strings ring as long as possible when playing fingerstyle.

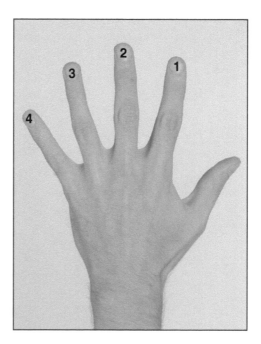

Can't Help Falling in Love

from the Paramount Picture BLUE HAWAII

Words and Music by George David Weiss, Hugo Peretti and Luigi Creatore

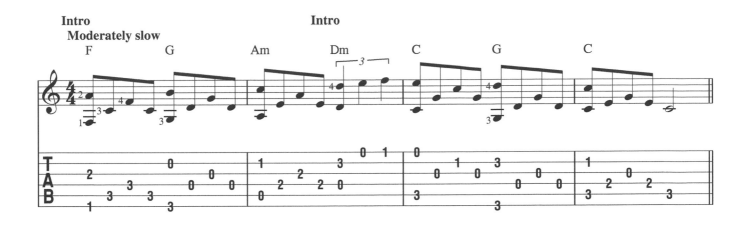

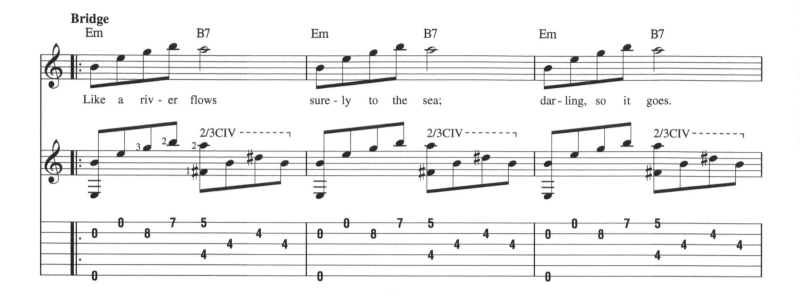

Bridge

Like a riv-er flows sure-ly to the sea; dar-ling, so it goes.

Verse

Some things ___ are meant to be. 3., 4. Take my

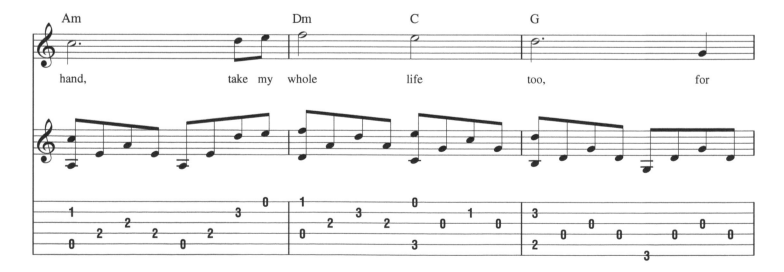

hand, take my whole life too, for

I can't help fall-ing in love with you.

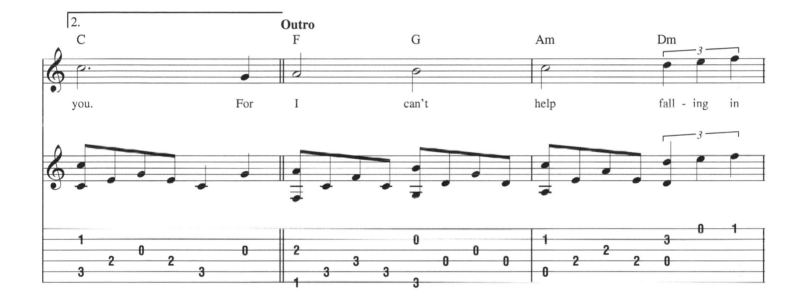

you. For I can't help fall-ing in

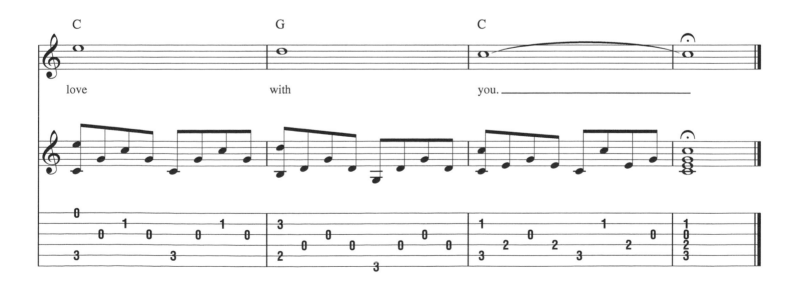

love with you.

Fly Me to the Moon

(In Other Words)

featured in the Motion Picture ONCE AROUND

Words and Music by Bart Howard

In oth - er words,   darl - ing kiss me.

Verse

2. Fill my heart with song___ and let me sing for-ev - er

more.   You are all I long for, all I

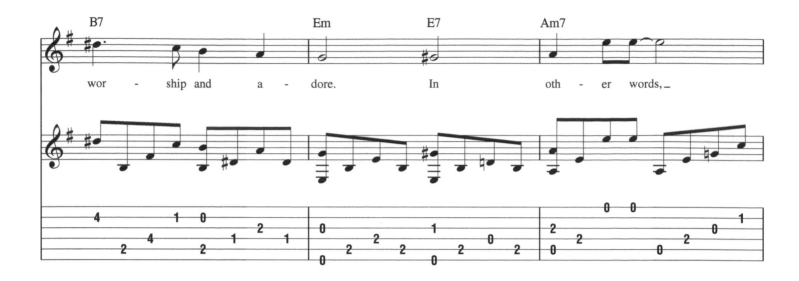

wor - ship and a - dore. In oth - er words,

please be true, in oth - er words,

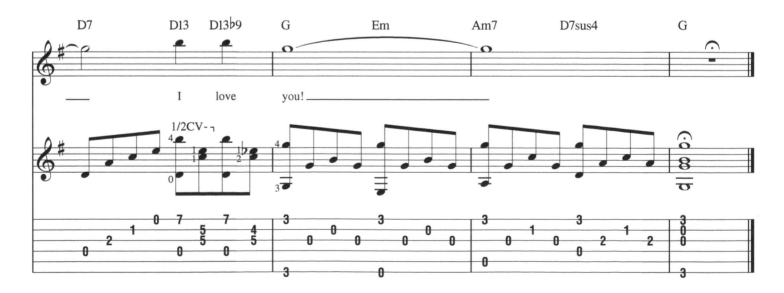

I love you!

I Just Called to Say I Love You

Words and Music by Stevie Wonder

no song to sing.
is some-thing true,

In fact here's just an-oth — er
made up of these three words_ that

or-di-nar-y day.
I must say to

2. No A — pril you:

I just

Chorus

called _____ to say _____ I love _____ you.

I just called _____ to

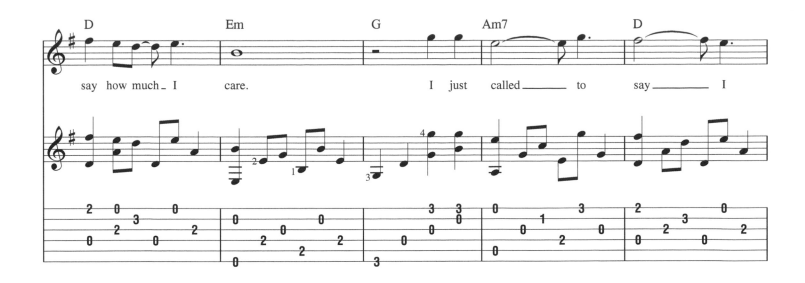

say how much _ I care.   I just called _____ to say _____ I

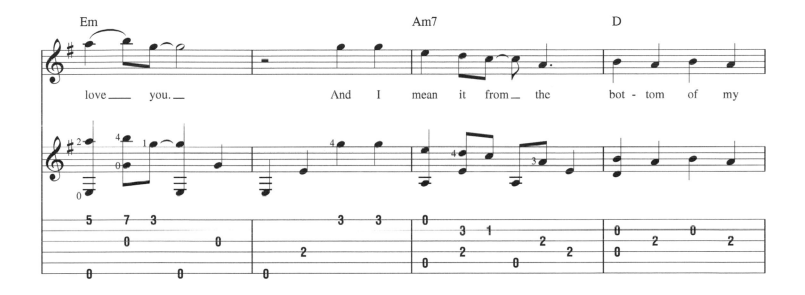

love ____ you. ____   And I mean it from _ the   bot - tom of my

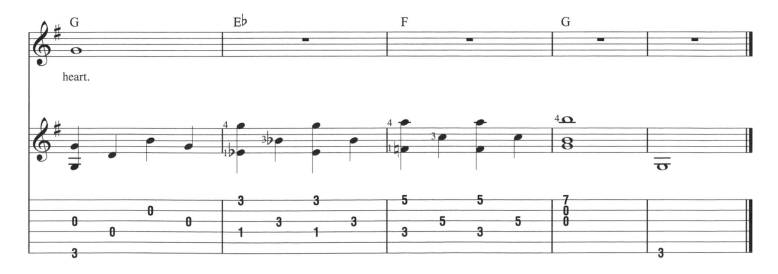

heart.

Georgia on My Mind

Words by Stuart Gorrell
Music by Hoagy Carmichael

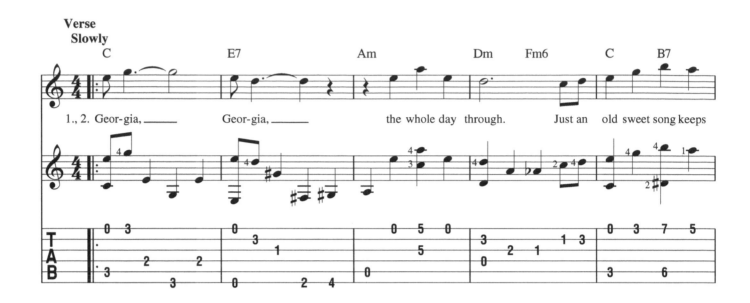

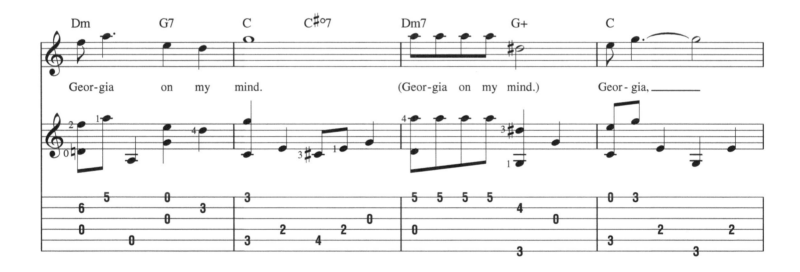

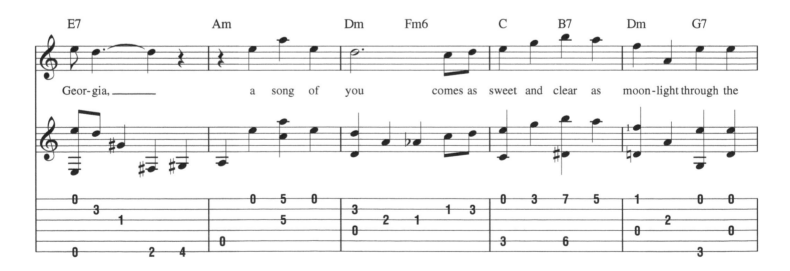

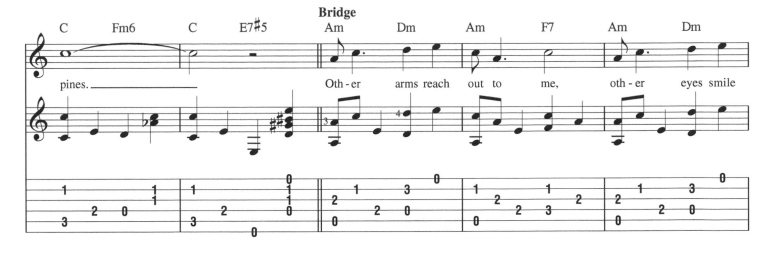

Bridge

pines. _____ Oth-er arms reach out to me, oth-er eyes smile

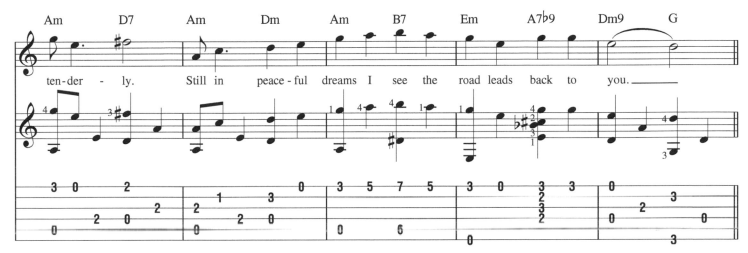

ten-der - ly. Still in peace-ful dreams I see the road leads back to you. _____

Outro

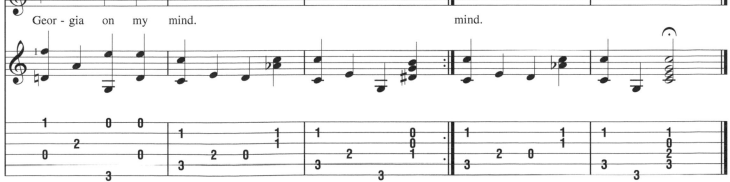

Geor-gia, _____ Geor-gia, _____ no peace I find, just an old sweet song keeps

Geor - gia on my mind. mind.

I Could Write a Book

from PAL JOEY

Words by Lorenz Hart
Music by Richard Rodgers

simple se-cret of the plot _____ is just to tell them that I love you a

lot. _____ Then the world dis - cov-ers as my book ends, how to

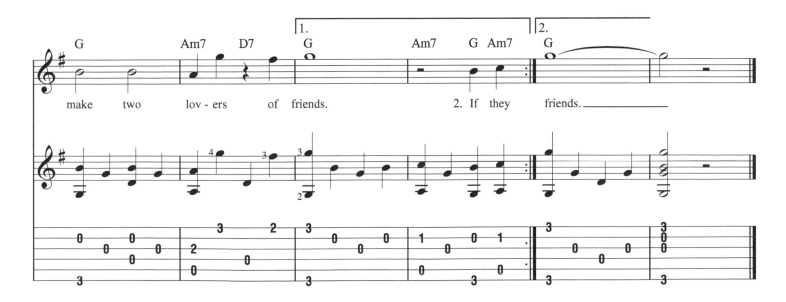

make two lov-ers of friends. 2. If they friends. _____

I've Grown Accustomed to Her Face

from MY FAIR LADY

Words by Alan Jay Lerner
Music by Frederick Loewe

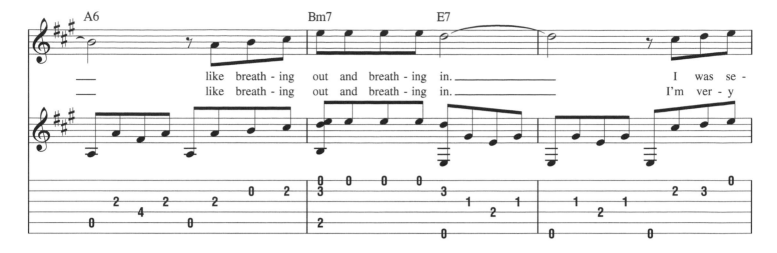

like breath-ing out and breath-ing in. ____ I was se-
like breath-ing out and breath-ing in. ____ I'm ver-y

rene-ly in-de-pen-dent and con-tent be-fore we met; sure-ly I could al-ways be that
grate-ful she's a wom-an and so eas-y to for-get; rath-er like a hab-it one can

way a-gain and yet, I've grown ac-cus-tomed to her looks; ac-cus-tomed to her voice; ac-
al-ways break and yet, I've grown ac-cus-tomed to the trace of some-thing in the air; ac-

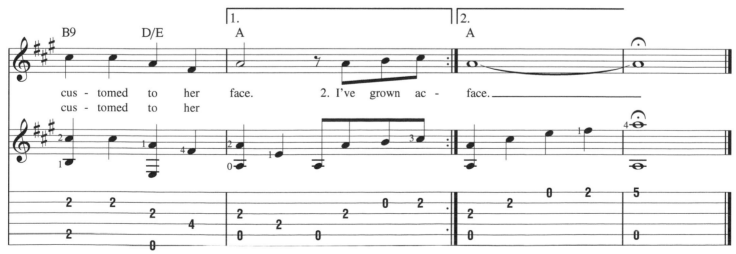

cus-tomed to her face. 2. I've grown ac- face. ____
cus-tomed to her

In a Sentimental Mood

Words and Music by Duke Ellington, Irving Mills and Manny Kurtz

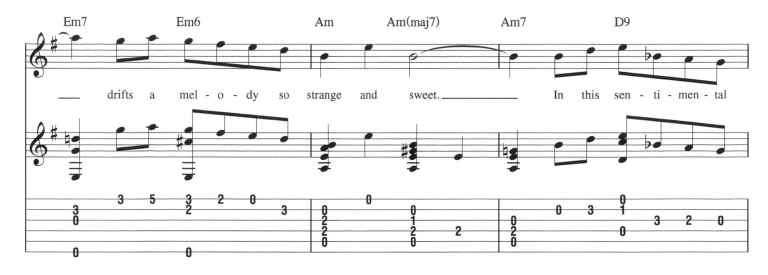

Bridge

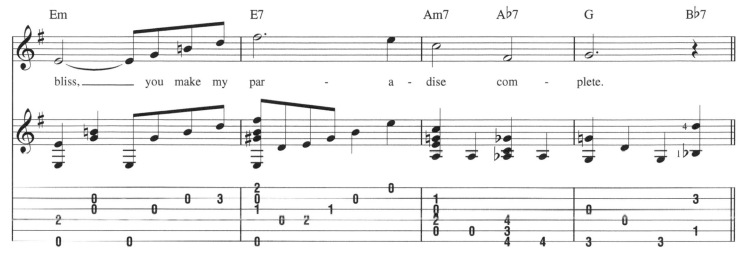

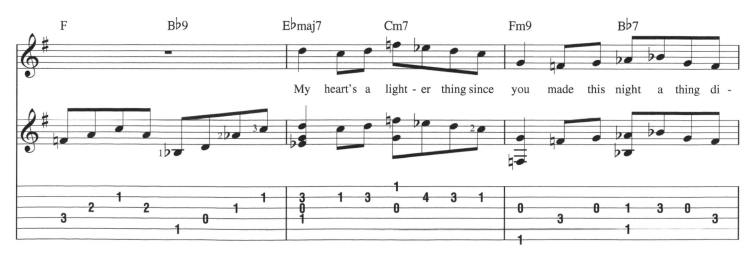

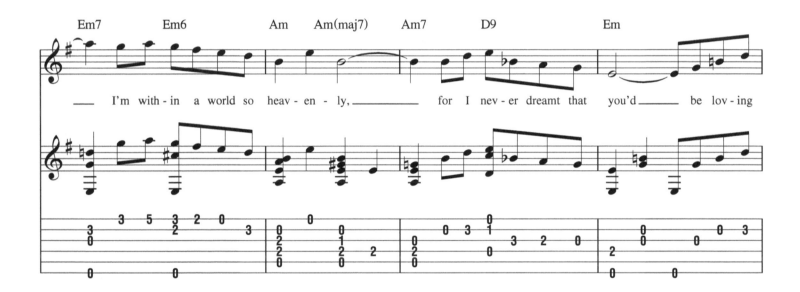

Just the Way You Are

Words and Music by Billy Joel

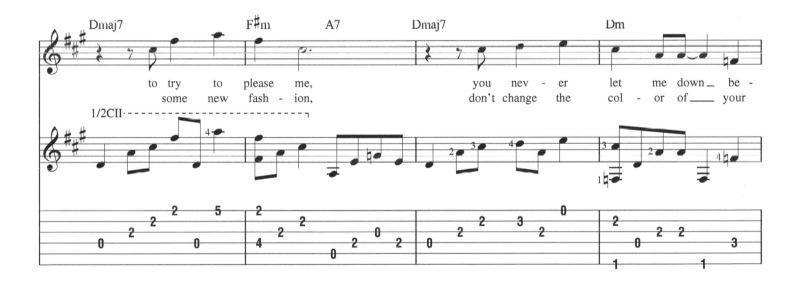

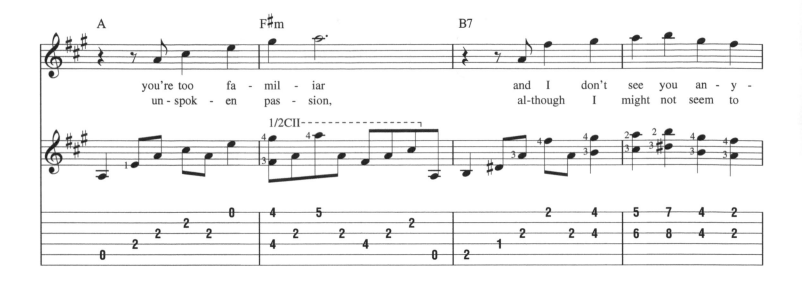

you're too fa - mil - iar
un - spok - en pas - sion,

and I don't see you an - y -
al-though I might not seem to

more.
care.

I would not leave you
I don't want clev - er
said I love you

in times of trou - ble,
con - ver - sa - tion,
and that's for - ev - er,

we nev - er could have come this
I nev - er want to work that
and this I prom - ise from the

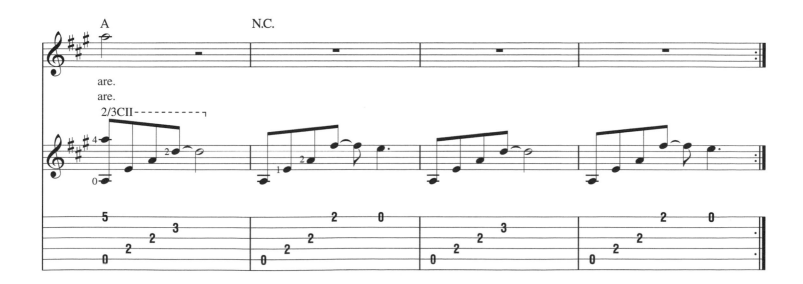

Bridge

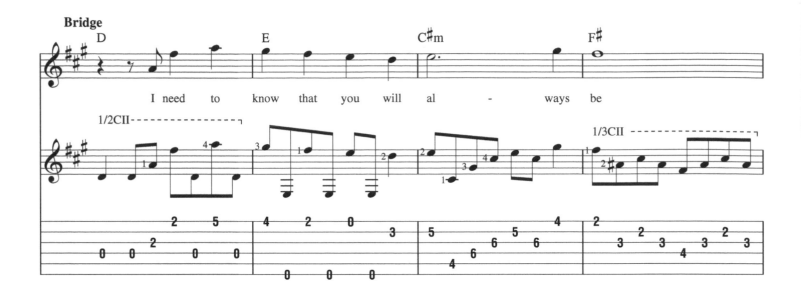

I need to know that you will al - ways be

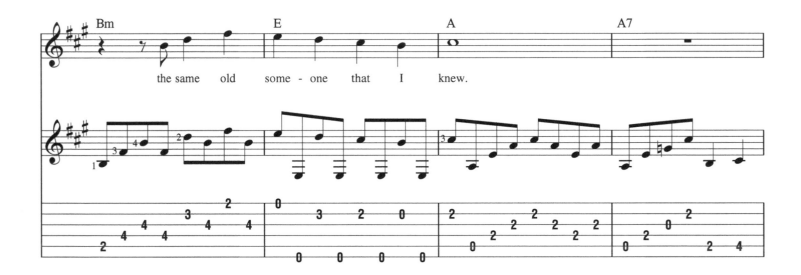

the same old some - one that I knew.

What will it take till you be - lieve in me

the way that I be - lieve in you?   I ___

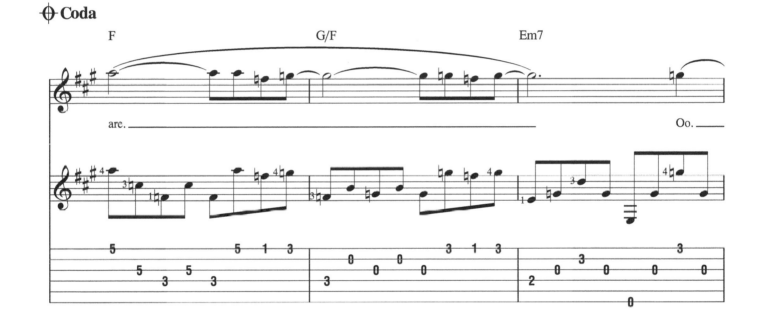

Coda

F   G/F   Em7

are. ___   Oo. ___

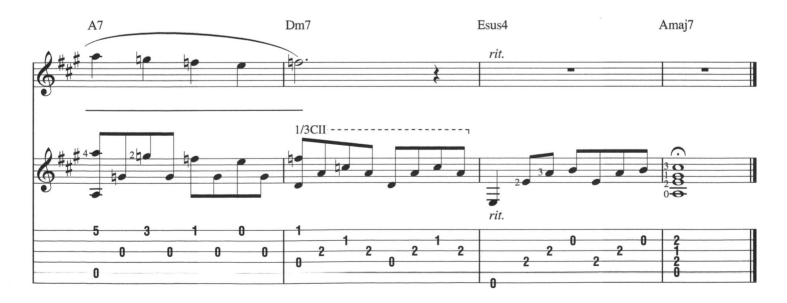

A7   Dm7   Esus4   Amaj7

rit.

Misty

Words by Johnny Burke
Music by Erroll Garner

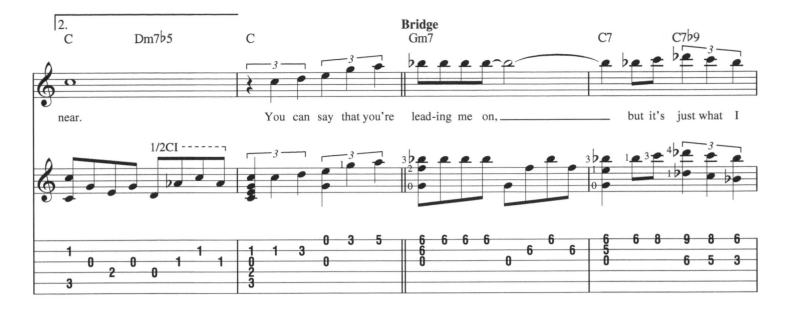

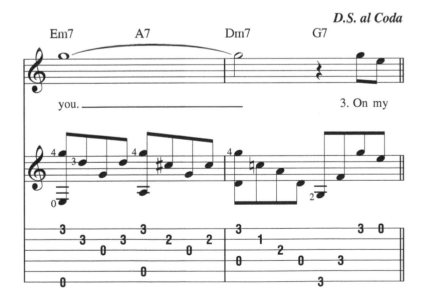

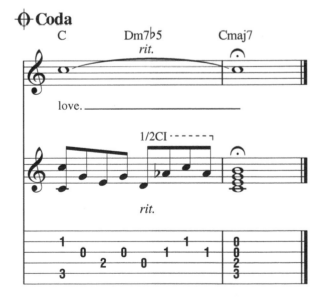

Additional Lyrics

2. Walk my way,
   And a thousand violins begin to play,
   Or it might be the sound of your hello,
   That music I hear,
   I get misty the moment you're near.

3. On my own,
   Would I wander through this wonderland alone,
   Never knowing my right foot from my left,
   My hat from my glove?
   I'm too misty and too much in love.

Moon River

from the Paramount Picture BREAKFAST AT TIFFANY'S

Words by Johnny Mercer
Music by Henry Mancini

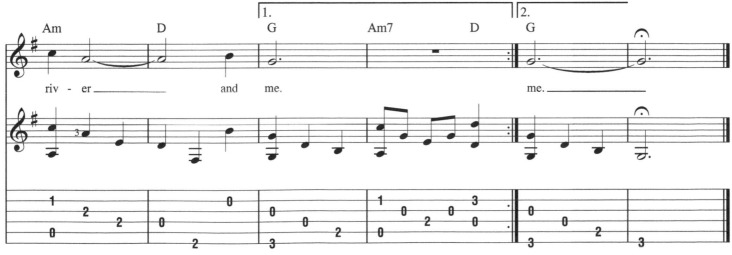

My Favorite Things

from THE SOUND OF MUSIC

Lyrics by Oscar Hammerstein II
Music by Richard Rodgers

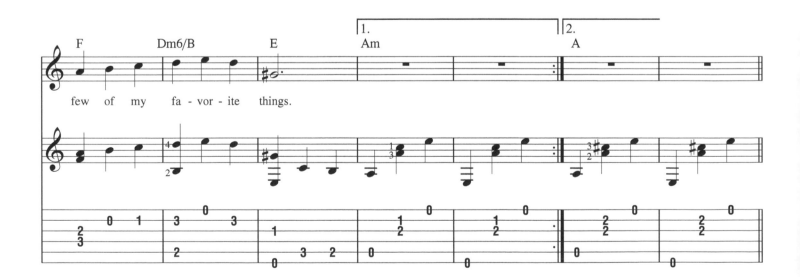

3. Girls in white dress - es with blue sat - in sash - es, snow-flakes that stay on my nose and eye -

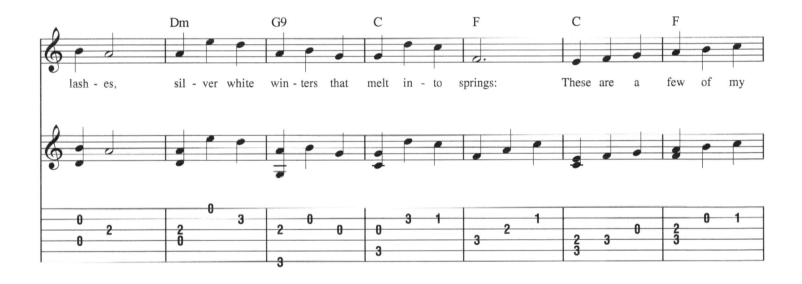

lash - es, sil - ver white win - ters that melt in - to springs: These are a few of my

Bridge

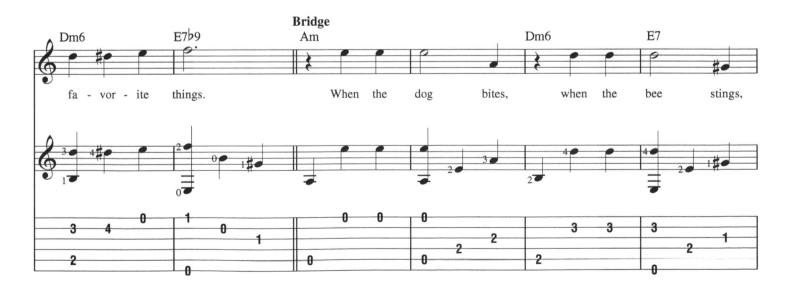

fa - vor - ite things. When the dog bites, when the bee stings,

when I'm feel - ing sad, _____ I sim - ply re - mem - ber my

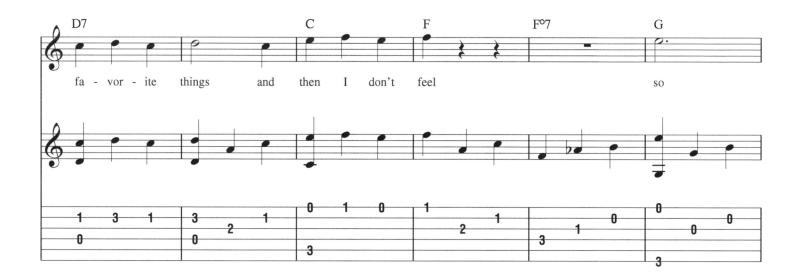

fa - vor - ite things and then I don't feel so

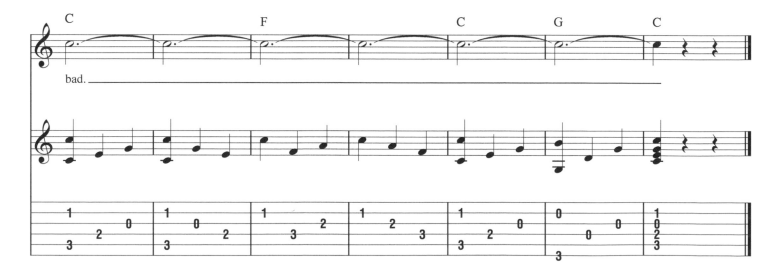

bad. _____

Unchained Melody

from the Motion Picture UNCHAINED

Lyric by Hy Zaret
Music by Alex North

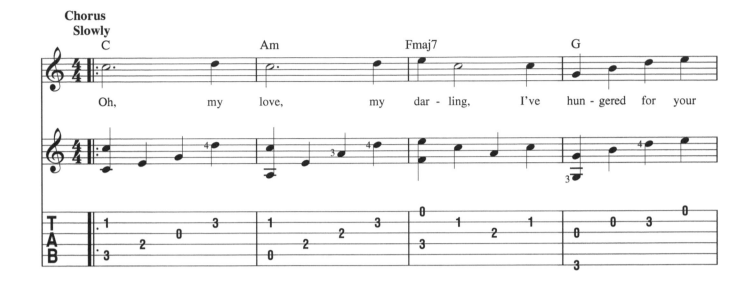

Oh, my love, my dar-ling, I've hun-gered for your

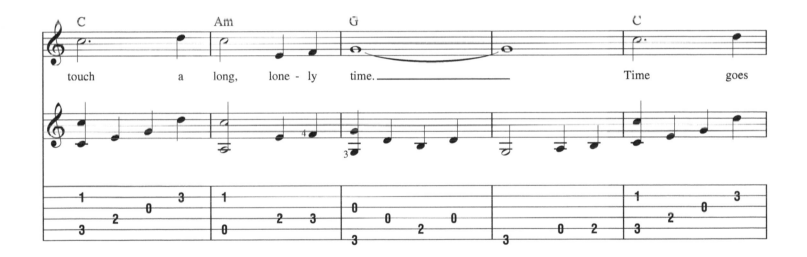

touch a long, lone-ly time. Time goes

by so slow-ly and time can do so much. Are you still

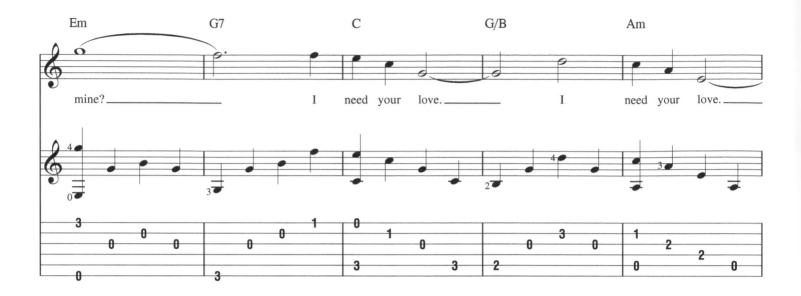

mine? _____ I need your love. _____ I need your love. _____

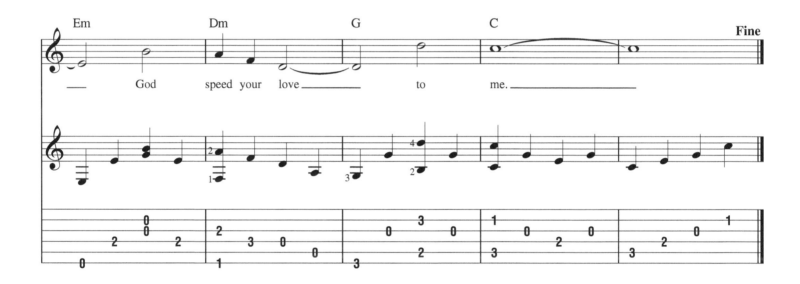

___ God speed your love _____ to me. _____

Fine

Bridge

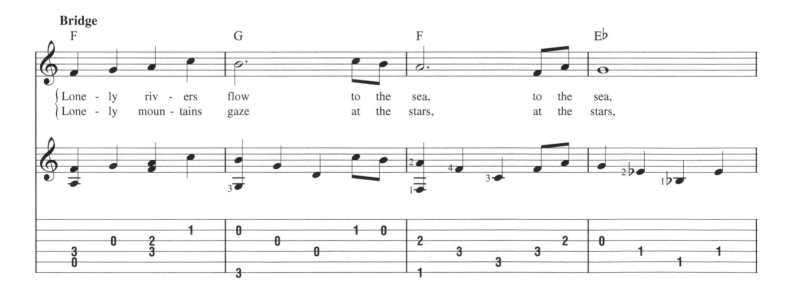

Lone - ly riv - ers flow to the sea, to the sea,
Lone - ly moun - tains gaze at the stars, at the stars,

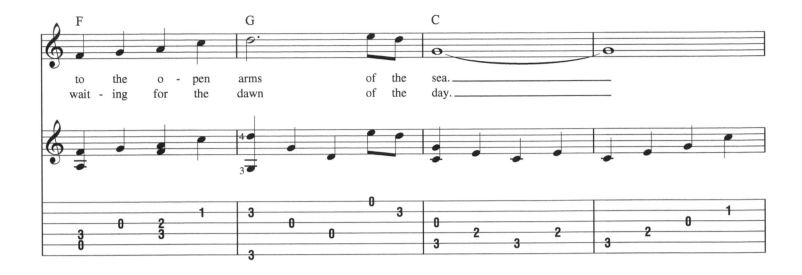

to the o - pen arms of the sea._____
wait - ing for the dawn of the day._____

Lone - ly riv - ers sigh, "Wait for me, wait for me!
All a - lone I gaze at the stars, at the stars,

I'll be com - ing home, wait for me!"_____
dream - ing of my love far a - way._____

The Way We Were

from the Motion Picture THE WAY WE WERE

Words by Alan and Marilyn Bergman
Music by Marvin Hamlisch

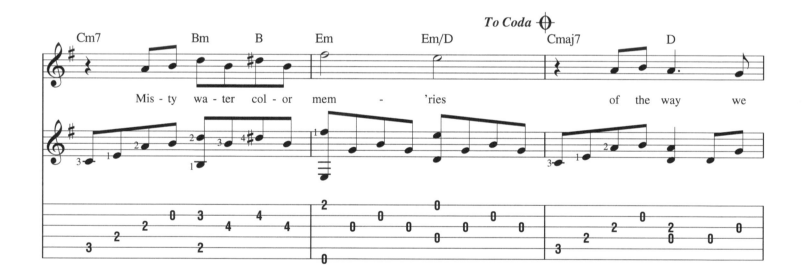

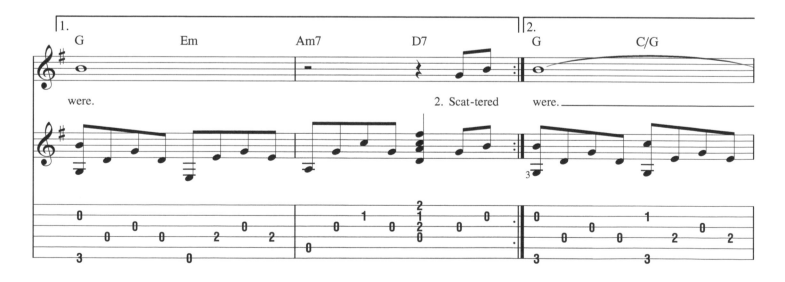

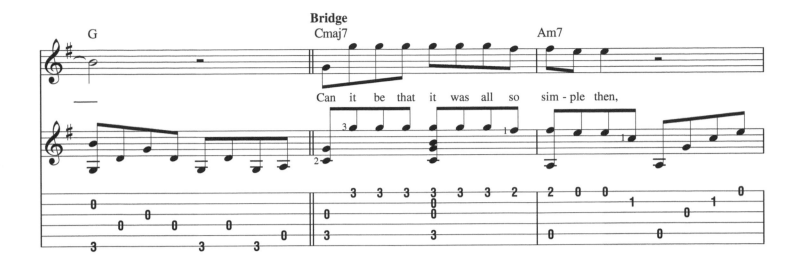

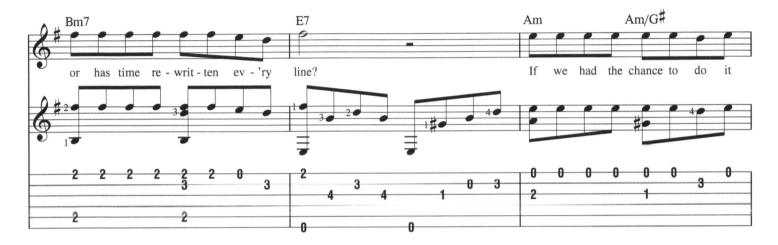

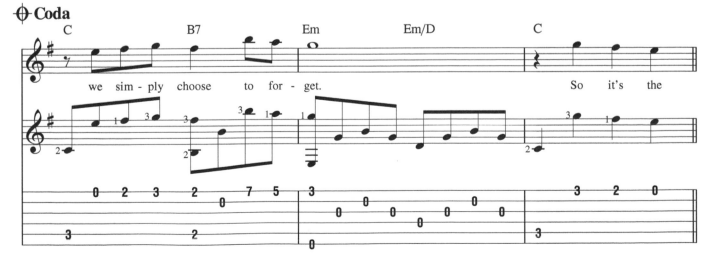

Outro

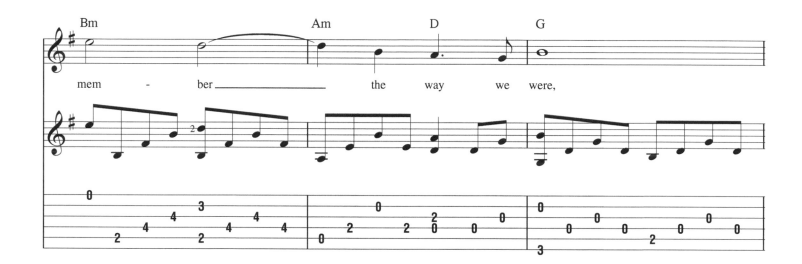

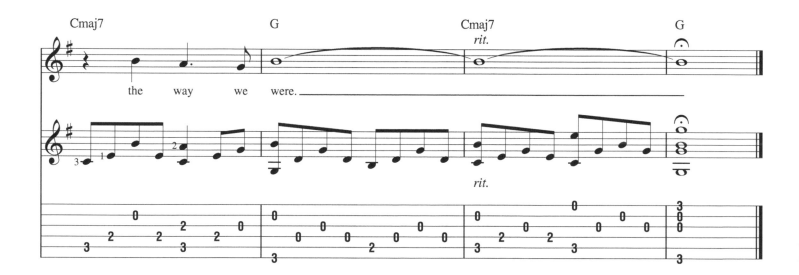

Additional Lyrics

2. Scattered pictures of the smiles we left behind;
   Smiles we gave to one another
   For the way we were.

3. Memories may be beautiful and yet,
   What's too painful to remember,
   We simply choose to forget.

What a Wonderful World

Words and Music by George David Weiss and Bob Thiele

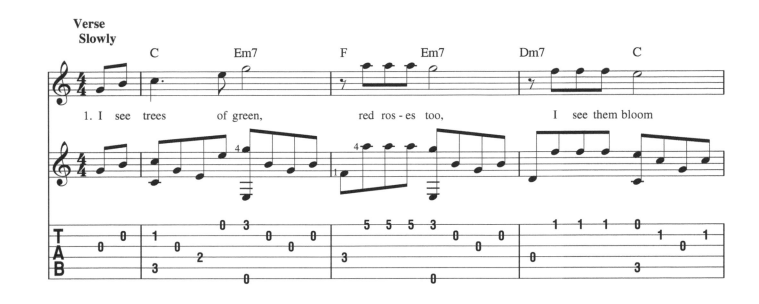

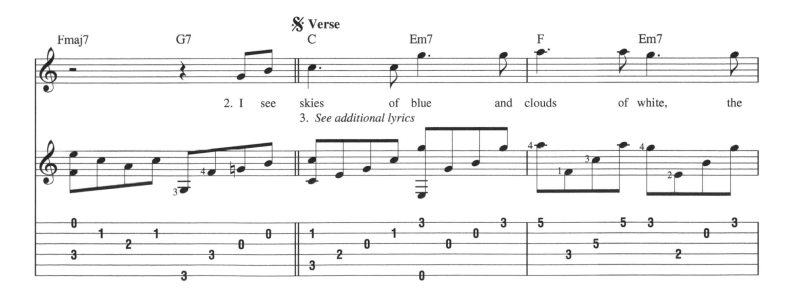

To Coda ⊕

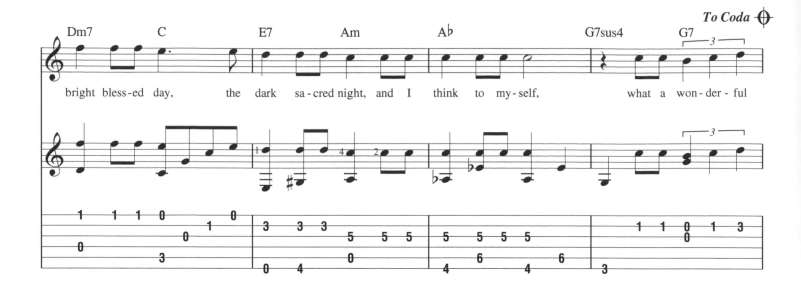

bright bless-ed day, the dark sa-cred night, and I think to my-self, what a won-der-ful

Bridge

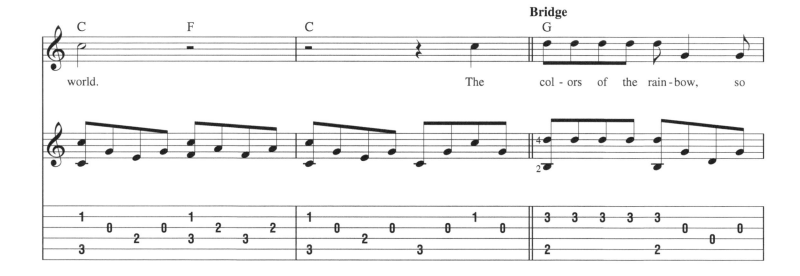

world. The col-ors of the rain-bow, so

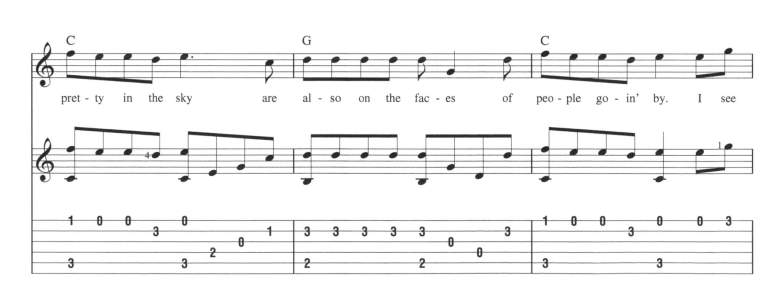

pret-ty in the sky are al-so on the fac-es of peo-ple go-in' by. I see

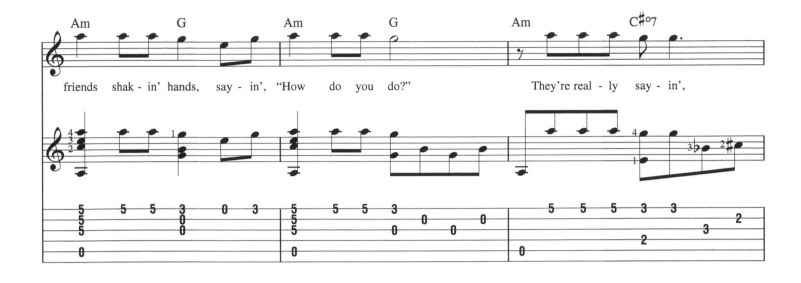

friends shak - in' hands, say - in', "How do you do?" They're real - ly say - in',

♦ Coda

D.S. al Coda

"I love you." 3. I hear

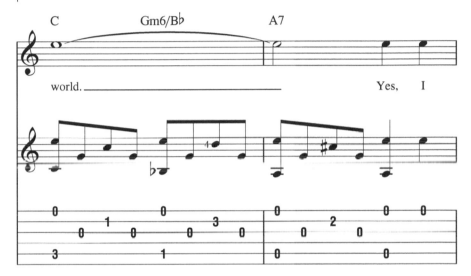

world. _____ Yes, I

think to my - self what a won - der - ful world.

Additional Lyrics

3. I hear babies cry, I watch them grow;
   They'll learn much more than I'll ever know.
   And I think to myself, what a wonderful world.
   Yes, I think to myself, what a wonderful world.

When I Fall in Love

Words by Edward Heyman
Music by Victor Young

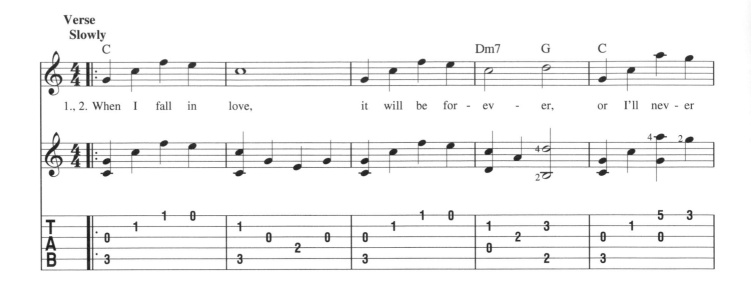

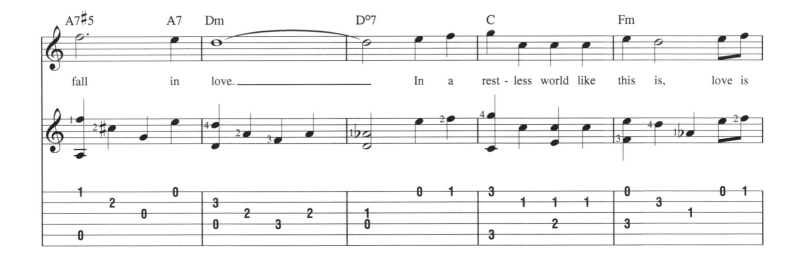

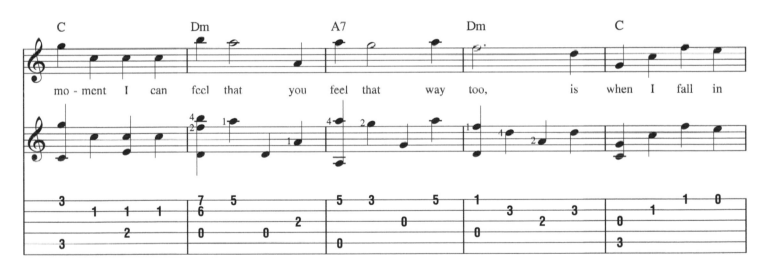

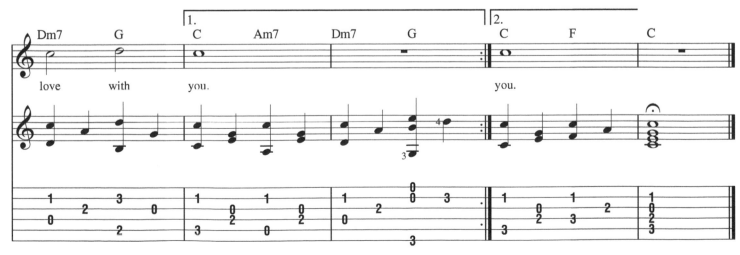

You Are So Beautiful

Words and Music by Billy Preston and Bruce Fisher

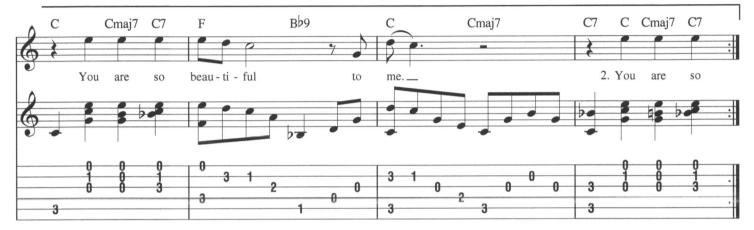

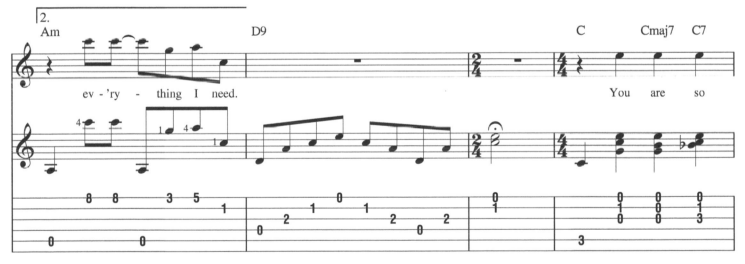

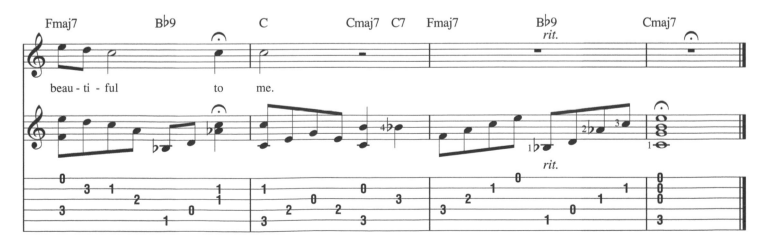

Yesterday

Words and Music by John Lennon and Paul McCartney

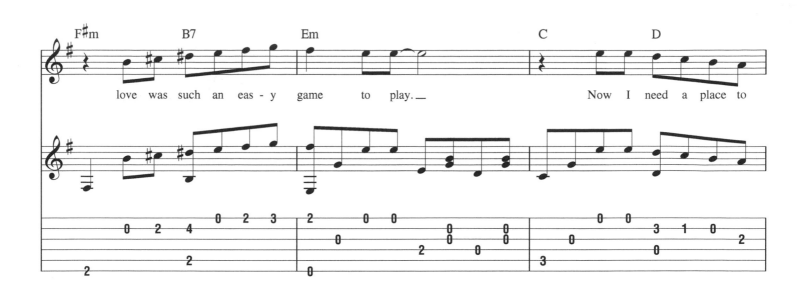

love was such an eas - y game to play. Now I need a place to

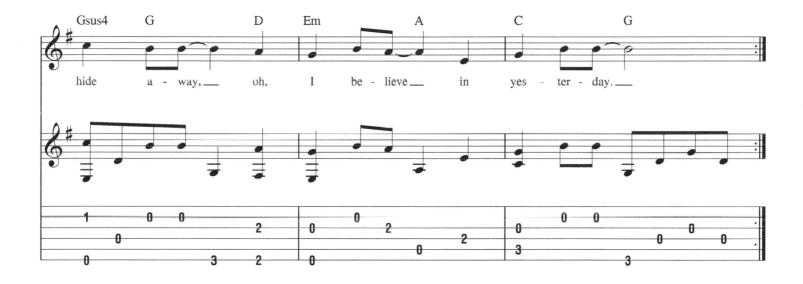

hide a - way, oh, I be - lieve in yes - ter - day.

Outro

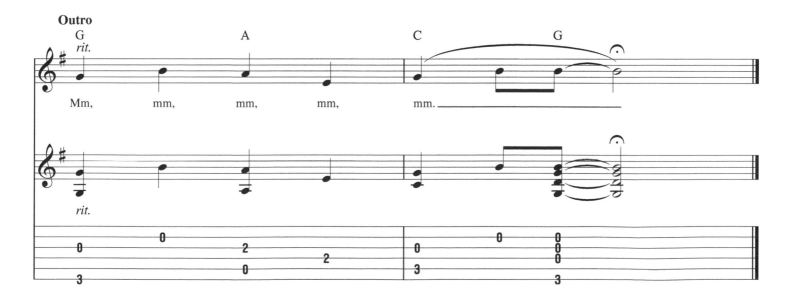

Mm, mm, mm, mm, mm.

48

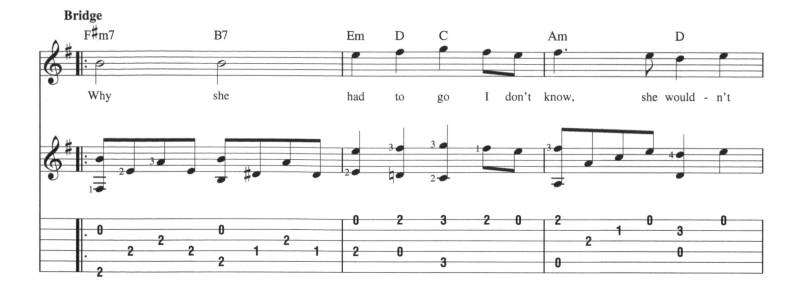

Bridge

Why she had to go I don't know, she would-n't

say. I said some - thing wrong, now I

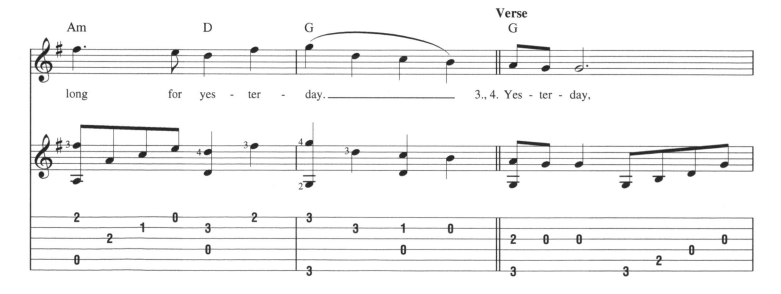

long for yes - ter - day. _____ 3., 4. Yes - ter - day,

Verse